TESTIMONIALS

"I find that using these TOOLS helps me nourish and maintain my spiritual consciousness. Now these TOOLS are internally available to me, anytime, even when I catch myself being out of balance, which is becoming less and less frequent."

— Evelyn Jacobs-Madrid, RN, Coordinator,

Faith Community Nursing

"I had become aware of my spirituality before I encountered the TOOLS, and had slowly progressed in my learning over about 20 years, but had come to a lull where things were okay, just not advancing."

"Several years ago, I began using the TOOLS, and right from the first day of using TOOL #1, I could see the benefits. I no longer fought myself, I got things done faster, more peacefully, more joyfully, and more decisively. I even stopped being afraid of losing my job."

"I continue to see improvements in my relationships, my intuition, and my insightfulness."

— Barry Morris,

Quality Control, aerospace industry

"I was raised in a religious environment that praised and accepted those that performed the 'right' behaviors, regardless of what not-so-good thoughts they might have had.. I felt not 'spiritual' enough, because my behavior did not fully conform, even though my thoughts were okay. After learning and applying the TOOLS, I have discovered that I am a lot more spiritual than I thought. My intuition, peace, and joy are better than ever. Most significant was when my Nurse Practitioner said, "What are you doing different? You're a lot happier, now." She's right! That was two years ago, and I continue to, not only maintain my spiritual gains, but to make new ones."

—Barbara Caldwell, M.D. family practice

A REDISCOVERY OF FREE WILL

AN UN-DOING

FREDERICK J. SMITH, MD

Y-OUR Spirituality Center, Inc.

Cover design by T J Publish, www.tjpublish.com

ISBN979-8-218-63619-7

LCCN: 2025904906

Disclaimer and Reader Agreement

Reader Agreement for Accessing This Book

Printed in the United States of America

Contents

PREFACE

FREE WILL

FREE. FREE WILL. FREE TO DO. FREEDOM. FREEDOM TO DO. FREEDOM FROM.

There is a nagging sense in the contemplation of free will that there is less of it than we had before. There is also an underlying anxiety that next week we may have less than we have today.

Unfortunately, attempts at discovering where it went have been elusive, and attempts at recovering it have proven unrewarding.

This work is an exploration of these very two processes.

The next two sections will explore where our free will went, first from a universal point of view, and then from a human perspective.

What follows are specific tools and lessons for the recovery of free will in the process of rediscovery, an un-doing.

This is an adventure in first unbuilding of that which depletes our free will, then the strengthening that which promotes our free will.

Since there are a great number of details that have accumulated over time that would be best un-done, it is necessary to be patient going through these lessons. We will begin by rebuilding the foundation, figuratively, of a multi-story building, starting in the basement.

There will be the temptation while beginning to learn in the basement, to want to move from floor to floor and to explore what is there. This is only human. This is a process and processes take time.

Laying the groundwork is essential to the steps that follow.

Each TOOL represents an un-doing of an aspect. Therefore, it is recommended that each TOOL be applied for THREE WEEKS OR MORE, in order to give the best opportunity to fully test its value for you.

Come, then, and join me in the satisfying adventure of:

A REDISCOVERY OF FREE WILL

INTRODUCTION

A REDISCOVERY OF FREE WILL

The mystics of the past taught, and the mystics and spiritual teachers of the present still teach, many things, on many levels. Sometimes, they addressed the physical/material levels, sometimes the magical, and at other times, the spiritual/metaphysical realm.

They taught with a huge variety of non-vocabulary techniques, for example, they used sounds of nature, some real, some imitated. They fasted, practiced personal denial, and utilized pain and endurance.

Those techniques that did use vocabulary, utilized stories, parables, imagery, metaphor, chant, and song to convey their point.

Most of what they attempted to teach could not be taught in simple conversation form, because there was not enough vocabulary to do it, and not enough group experience with the vocabulary available to provide a good frame of reference. So ceremony, ritual, and experiencing were the tools that often replaced intellectual instruction.

Although we have a rich vocabulary today in our society, compared to antiquity, we still have marked limitations when it comes to conveying spiritual or mystical concepts. In addition to learning a thing intellectually, it must also be learned experientially, emotionally, and even physically. Also, an important piece to learning, is the teaching of it. These latter will continue to be necessary no matter what, and these will still have as the extra function, at present, of propping up that portion of our intellectual instruction for which we have not yet developed vocabulary.

All mystics and spiritual teachers (the good guys, not the bad), by their efforts, always strive to increase awareness in their pupils, which also causes change in levels of vibration in them, which in turn leads to their heightened experiencing.

By looking at the efforts of those teachers in light of today's vocabulary, we can identify several principles taught, that seem to have been true of all these disciplines, and now can describe them.

One of these, "Know thyself", or some variation of this instruction, whether stated or merely implied, seemed to produce a focus on the following points:

1) **Become aware of your thoughts**. It is currently estimated that the average person has in the range of 60,000 thoughts each day, including both the conscious and the sub-conscious. Most are sub-conscious, below the level of conscious awareness, but easily accessible;

2) **Become aware of the content of your thoughts**. If you were aware of the content of many of your fear-based thoughts, you would not even allow them in. You allowed them in the first place because they were disguised as something better than they were, then they were moved to the sub-conscious;

3) **Become aware of the effects of your thoughts**. The effects of your thoughts can cause your body to be light and energetic, or heavy and slow, promote illness or health, nurture your relationships or destroy them. It all begins with thought, and the sub-conscious thoughts are important in this;

4) **Become aware that thoughts are choices**. Choose your next thought, or choose to delete the last one. Develop the habit of choice for your current thoughts. It takes some practice;

5) **Choose the thoughts with which to fill the empty spaces left by the thoughts you removed.** If you do not fill the space with what you want, it will be filled with something else, by default.

6) **Choose your focus.** The above five disciplines will work equally well in business, hobbies, sports, child rearing, or in the development of spirituality as one of the good guys.

By encountering these principles now, and by having a beginning understanding of them as a foundation, the student or pupil in pursuit of enlightenment will shorten the time, and streamline the effort, and possibly avoid some detours on the journey.

PART ONE
THE COSMIC PROBLEM: A DOING

Somehow we came into being. We seem to have some elements of free will. The circumstances under which that happened are something about which we have limited understanding, to say the least.

Perhaps a useful construct is to use a modified biblical account. It is a way to look at this that is useful for me, and conceptually fits, even though the details are open to debate.

In the beginning there was God. All-knowing. All-present. All-loving. All-powerful. All. But there was nothing else to apply all that to, except to God. There was no other thing or being to know, to love, and no demonstration of power, or wisdom, and nothing to experience. So, God decided to create 17 trillion beings, or so. Then they could experience the All, including getting to know each other. Then God created the physical universe. It doesn't matter whether it was done quickly or slowly, or whether the 17 trillion or so participated in the decision or the initiation of it.

Then God said to the 17 trillion or so, this physical universe is a playground. It is a carnival. You can go into it, scare yourselves or delight yourselves in any way or manner you can conceive. I promise you that you will always be safe, even though you may imagine that you are not.

You may fold, spindle, mutilate, distort, or warp your spirit as much as you desire. You will reach a point where you will decide that you have had enough. You will want to return home, even though you are likely not to remember exactly where you came from. As soon as you are ready, guidance will be available to you, in various forms.

In the process of returning, all the folding, spindling, mutilating, distorting, and warping of your spirit must be undone, and returned to its original state. I do not Will that any be lost.

Now, God said, do any of you want to go play?

And nearly all of us said YES! In doing so, we found that we could experience either through joy, which cost us little or nothing, or we could experience through fear, in which some of our free will is lost. Some of the fear experiences cost us more free will than others. Once we did some of the "doing", especially that which we did through fear, we could not go back and experience the oneness with God that we had before, without some "un-doing".

Some will decide to begin the un-doing earlier than others. Some will continue to experience one carnival ride after another for a very long time. This will create an ever increasing distortion that will eventually require un-doing.

PART TWO
THE HUMAN PROBLEM: A DOING

Picture a normal healthy infant. It has only basic responses, making sounds but no speech. It has a mind but no intellect. It has bodily functions but no control. It can be upset or at peace.

Let us discuss this peace.

When this infant is at peace, it is not worrying, not planning for tomorrow, not holding resentment, is not in the least upset.

Some people think, in this peaceful state, the infant is capable of giving and receiving love, and they are probably correct. It *is* also capable of joy, decisiveness, and related characteristics, as well.

Hold this image of peace in your mind, for it is this peaceful state of the infant I will be talking of in what follows.

It is the nature of the human condition that this child will experience various ways of being upset. The child will experience separation, being uncomfortable due to wetness, rash, hunger, and may even accidentally be pricked by a safety pin. It will be upset.

But as soon as the problem is resolved, it will return to peace.

After a few months, the child will begin to experience different degrees of upset-ness to various stimuli and different intensities of response.

When these stimuli are removed, it will return to peace.

Gradually, the child will begin to recognize situations that seem to have the potential to cause loss, harm or shortage, and will learn to be upset, even before anything adverse happens. The child will learn to be afraid.

But when the stimulus is re-moved, the child will return to peace.

The child has now learned in a basic way about loss, harm and shortages, and that it does not want them.

When those things are not pres-ent, the child returns to peace, which is its natural state.

Although parents and other care-givers recognize the existence of this peaceful state, they do not fully understand this peace. They no longer routinely experience this peace, although they would like to. Their experience seems to have taught them this peace is inevitably lost through 'growing up.' Now these well-meaning people decide to 'improve' this child, by teaching it the correct ways to be upset and afraid, in order to more successfully 'cope with the real world.'

They add advanced learning to the basic upsets the child has already learned. They teach it more fear. They teach guilt, fear of abandonment, loss of self esteem, loss of the good will of other people, fear of not doing it right, not doing enough, not doing it on time, fear of shame, and fear of death.

They teach a wide variety of responses and ways to be upset. They teach blaming, accusing, finding fault, condemning, and passing judgment.

Eventually, the child goes back to

peace only rarely, and then only
for brief periods.

New definitions are put in place,
all of them with some element
of fear. Now there are good fear
and bad fear. The good fears are
defined as your friends, the bad
fears as your enemies. Winning
is defined as not losing, and is
good. Losing is defined as not
winning, and is bad. Positive
thinking is defined as a struggle
against negative thinking.

Peace is now defined as what
is left over when most of your
problems are solved, while you
are waiting for the next problem
to appear. Acceptance of upset
in lesser amounts is now routine,
because dissolving all upset now
seems impossible. Everything
now seems defined by extremes
or dichotomies - good and bad,
tall and short, positive and negative, stress and ease, rich and
poor, right and wrong, all this
way or all that way.

The brain has now been fully
programmed as a problem-solv-
ing computer, which sees everything as a problem or a potential
problem.

Still, once in a while, the child
falls into the peace of a younger
time, has a 'hit' of joy, here and
there.

Then comes puberty, with its
initial sense of wonder.

Quickly, there comes the tendency for all the learning that
has gone before to be re-defined. Re-defined in terms of male/
female relationships. More turmoil. More challenges. More
opportunity to define life in terms of fear, loss, harm, shortages,
and especially guilt, social inadequacy and passing judgment.

> Peace now seems so remote, it is
> defined in terms of the elusive
> perfect relationship that might
> someday happen.
>
> Now, if you wanted to go back
> to that peace of early childhood,
> you would have little clue about
> how to do it.

Yet that peace is what we ultimately seek with our free will.

> All of our 'doing' is aimed at
> finding that lasting, sustaining
> peace.

There must be a better way, don't
you think?

PART THREE
TOOL #1: BUILDING A THOUGHT MONITOR

AN UN-DONG

There must be a better way.

What we have covered so far is merely a handful of the hundreds and even thousands of ways we have learned over time to upset ourselves. This is an example of successful behavior:

We started our journeys as children, laying a foundation, a little piece here, a little piece there, about how to react to our environment with fear, upset and, especially, guilty ways. Now we are adults, and we have built a system that thoroughly blocks our ability to visit that peace of childhood.

There is nothing wrong with our success mechanism!

We have merely discovered we have succeeded at something we no longer want.

Just as we have learned how to upset ourselves, we are able to learn other things. Also, we can un-learn things. Just as we may have learned bad habits as youngsters, we may have un-learned them by the time we became adults.

We can redirect our success mechanism! What you are about to learn is simple but requires persistence. Climbing a tall mountain is simple. You start at the bottom and proceed to the top. There may be some skills it would be wise to have mastered before beginning, but they do not require a college degree. Still, it requires persistence, even if the skills are mastered.

We are now at the top of a mountain, figuratively. Climbing

down is also simple, but it too requires persistence.

The skills you are about to learn could have been mastered in pre-school, if there had been someone there to teach them. It would have been easier to learn then than now. So much of what you learned since pre-school is opposite to this learning, so for many of you, it will feel foreign.

Just as your foundation was laid down starting in childhood with the mind of a child, at the level of the child, so too shall the un-doing of the foundation and its rebuilding begin at the level of the child ... at least briefly.

At this point, your adult mind will have a tendency to fight this information.

So, please put your adult mind on the shelf, so to speak, and listen with the openness of a child, so this will be more readily understood and received.

For now, decide not to criticize, evaluate, or problem-solve. Just practice and learn.

There are times when you are aware of thoughts and feelings while they occur; times when you are aware after the fact, and times when you are not aware at all. At the times when you are aware of thoughts and feelings *while* they are occurring, it is as though you are watching yourself or noticing yourself do some behavior or make some decision.

For example, you may have had an occasion to observe yourself being especially tender with a child. Or you might have noticed an unusual calmness about yourself while engaged in making a difficult decision. You may have watched yourself make an unusually skillful maneuver in a work environment or sports situation. You have had the experience of being aware of a part within yourself, functioning as a Noticer, an Observer or a Watcher, of another part of yourself that was functioning as a Do-er.

This function of Noticer, Watcher or Observer always seems to occur with a sense of calmness. When you then become upset, or even distracted, the awareness of the Noticer, the Watcher or the Observer seems to disappear.

Most people have had these interesting moments, but have been unaware of any value or significance to the process, nor have they given any thought to promoting or utilizing this process for anything else.

Now it is time to assign a task to this Noticer, this Observer, this Watcher.

It is a simple task, which the Noticer could have performed for us while we were pre-school age, but a task that requires attention and focus by the individual, as well. The task assigned to this Noticer is the task of monitoring thoughts. Every thought you have is made up of either upset or peace, or some combination of the two. The Thought Monitor's task is merely to notice which it is.

Examples of thoughts on the peaceful side might be peace, love or joy.

Examples on the upset side might be upset, fear, anger or distraction.

Choose one word that you resonate with from each side, now, and remember it for later.

Every mental experience is made up of a single thought, paired or combined thoughts, or 'broken thoughts.'

An explanation about 'broken thoughts' is in order. Not everybody has 'broken thoughts.' These are thoughts that seem to come from out of nowhere, do not match the circumstances, and are very intense. Examples are panic attacks, manic-depressive disorder and rage attacks, which may be chemical malfunctions in the brain caused by genetic abnormalities or injury. Symptoms may range from intense fear to uncontrolled sobbing, to rage, and may be triggered by a good event, a bad event, a neutral event, or by no apparent event at all. There is often a sense of hopelessness about this.

While 'broken thoughts' are beyond the scope of this course, they can be successfully treated. There are specialists in the medical profession who are very good at treating and eliminating, or at least, greatly reducing the number of these events, and should be consulted.

One of my friends had secret 'broken thoughts' for many years, but was still able to maintain his law practice. He coped by developing an effective 'game face,' and concentrated an intense focus on the task at hand, forcefully pushing the 'broken thoughts' into the background. Eventually, his health began to deteriorate, he could no longer maintain his law practice, and lost it. He began receiving medical care, saw the appropriate specialists, received medications, and the 'broken thoughts' began to reduce in number, intensity, and duration. They became rare. Hopelessness was gone.

This course can effectively deal with your *reaction* to these 'broken thoughts.' People often react with guilt, hopelessness, low self-esteem, and helplessness over these 'broken thoughts'. There is hope. If you discover this problem within yourself, please tell someone, and find out where to get additional help.

Now, back to Tool #1: BUILDING A THOUGHT MONITOR.

Once each hour, while awake, over the next three weeks, take a moment or two to randomly monitor your thoughts as to whether they are peaceful or upsetting. That is all.

Why three weeks? Two reasons. It takes about three weeks to begin to form a habit, and for it to begin to be easier. And, after three weeks, you can be confident you gave the project a good trial.

Please do not try to fix the upsetting thoughts. Why not? There are three reasons:

1) Fixing the upsetting thoughts will change focus away from building the Thought Monitor, and interfere with its development. Remember, this is best learned with the mind set of a child, not the mind of a master fixer.

2) You will try to fix the thoughts with your old methods, which have not been too successful in promoting your free will. (I will give you another tool later with which to fix things when the Thought Monitor has become a habit).

3) Perhaps the most important reason is, I want you to have the wonderful feeling that comes with the experience of seeing your upsetting thoughts disappear, without effort. If you knew how many of your thoughts were upsetting, you would not allow them. Most of these come in disguise, seeming to be your friends, and seeming to provide you some benefit by showing you the correct way to be angry or upset or insulted or guilty, without ever once hinting there might be a peaceful thought as an alternative. When the disguise comes off, the upsetting thought will most often disappear because its influence will be lost.

Most of the thoughts you monitor will be upsetting ones. That's all right. Even if you only have one, two, or three peaceful thoughts in a week, you are reasonably in balance. If you notice a peaceful one, celebrate it. Over time, as you double and triple the number and more, you will find yourself feeling more free, and then behaving more freely will follow.

Here is where you choose a word
that represents the peaceful side.
Choose from among the following: peaceful, loving, joyful.

And one from the upsetting side.
Choose from: fearful, angry, upsetting, distracting.

Set up an hourly 'trigger' for yourself. If your wristwatch has
an hourly chime on it, you might use that. If you watch TV a
lot, trigger your monitor at the program change. Some students
used, as their trigger, walking through a doorway. A pregnant
lady used the occasion of urinary urge, which had become hourly.
A grocery checker triggered every time she scanned bananas.
There are many other possible triggers, so use your imagination
to find the one that suits you best.

When the trigger happens, re-capture the thought that came
immediately *before* the trigger, to apply the Thought Monitor
to. This will ensure the thoughts chosen during this habit-build-
ing period are truly random. True randomness will help you
become aware that the littlest 'upsetting' thought will keep you
from being peaceful, joyful and loving, just as easily as a 'big'
upsetting thought.

It is better to let the trigger select the thought to monitor
than for you to try to pick which thoughts you want to address.

Let us imagine the example of having your trigger be 'walking
through a doorway,' because we imagine you routinely do that
on an average of once per hour, throughout the day.

You rise from your chair to go outdoors to get the mail, walk
through the front door, triggering your Thought Monitor, and
immediately ask yourself, "What was the thought just before
I walked through the doorway?" Then immediately ask the

question, "Was this a *peaceful* thought or an *upsetting* thought?" (using the words from each side *you* chose). Choose an answer and quickly move on, with no more attention than that.

Do this, or something like it, 12-14 times a day, while awake, for three weeks.

END OF WEEK ONE AFTER TOOL #1

PART THREE: TOOL #1: BUILDING A THOUGHT MONITOR

Building a habit requires focus, dedication, dealing with interruptions of both external and internal sources. It takes a minimum of three weeks just to begin to develop a habit.

It can be frustrating, or it can be an adventure.

Re-read the material daily, or more, if needed.

Re-affirm your chosen trigger. Re-evaluate it. Modify it if necessary.

Re-confirm that the word(s) you chose from the 'peaceful' side and the one(s) you chose from the 'upsetting' side are a good fit for you.

Re-commit to building a Thought Monitor.

Stay in touch with the Noticer, the Watcher, and the Observer.

Go to appendix A (starts on page 61) and select one article from those available to read for this week.

END OF WEEK TWO AFTER TOOL #1

Go back to the End of Week One. Re-read it, and re-evaluate again, noticing the advancements you have made, however small.

One more week to go, then you will reach a decision point.

Go to Appendix A and choose another article to read for this week.

Continue to build your Thought Monitor.

END OF WEEK THREE AFTER TOOL #1

Congratulations. You have completed the minimum necessary to finish the first stage of developing a new habit pattern.

There are a few questions that are best answered before continuing to the next tool, Tool. #2.

1) Have you experienced the Thought Monitor beginning to become habitual, i.e., are you triggering 12-14 times per day, and are thoughts being triggered spontaneously, *in addition* to the 12-14 programmed trigger times per day?

2) Have you experienced the disappearance of upsetting thoughts without any extra effort, just because they were noticed and identified?

3) Developing the Thought Monitor is essential for continuing the REDISCOVERY OF FREE WILL course, because the subsequent lessons use the Thought Monitor as a foundation. Do you want to continue to develop the Thought Monitor?

The above three questions should be answered in the affirmative before continuing. If you have answered 'YES' to them, please continue the course.

If you were not able to answer 'yes' right now, perhaps putting this course 'on the shelf' for the time being and returning to it at a later time would fit your needs.

For those of you who *are* continuing on, let us make the Thought Monitor a habit so firmly in place, it no longer requires your continued effort, and thus becomes automatic.

While I believe three weeks is the minimum for beginning to develop a habit such as this, many of my students have not felt comfortable moving on to the next tool, without spending more weeks in strengthening the Thought Monitor. That is perfectly all right, since this is not a timed course. The goal is to become good at it, not to compete with anyone else. The goal is to make the Thought Monitor a good and useful tool for you, and for it to become automatic.

Take a look at Tool. #2, to see if you are ready for it, or at one of the other tools. After the Thought Monitor is firmly in place, you can do the other tools in any order you want. If you do not feel proficient at 'monitoring' yet, continue your hourly practice until you feel comfortable enough to advance.

PART FOUR
TOOL #2A: CHALLENGE THE IDEA

AN UN-DOING

Welcome to Tool #2. Tool #2 is in three parts, A, B, and C.

Tool #2 is a method for dissolving more complex upsets than Tool #1. Typically, the reactions to working with Tool #1 over the previous several weeks have varied from one individual to another. Some will be astonished at how well it works. Others will remark on how easy it is. Some will be judgmental over how thoroughly they had fooled themselves.

Still others will experience feeling overwhelmed and unable to easily stop themselves from trying to 'fix' their thoughts.

Some will want to quit.

Most people become aware that some upsetting thoughts disappear effortlessly, while other thoughts seem to persist in spite of their efforts.

Most have asked themselves some form of the questions, "How did this happen?" "What did I do wrong?" "Have I inflicted so much damage on myself, I won't be able to turn this around?"

The answer is this: You have a perfectly intact success mechanism. After all, you have successfully learned all this upsetting programming, haven't you? Convincing the success mechanism part of your mind to focus in this new direction, and away from the previous direction, takes some time and some persistence. For the most part, it will become easy and automatic.

Tool #2A

Many people think their emotions are triggered as a stimulus/ response reaction, where the stimulus causes the response. For example, one person insults another, who automatically feels insulted.

But what if the second person doesn't hear the insult? Something has to happen in between the stimulus and the response. Let us explore this.

The first thing that must occur is perception. The next thing to realize is, perception is not just an instantaneous event, and it is coupled with an evaluation, before getting to the response.

STIMULUS   RESPONSE
(eg, insult)   (eg,anger)

PERCEPTION AND EVALUATION

(What happens in between)

"That's horrible terrible awful"	"That shouldn't happen" to me	"Anybody would get angry"	"Therefore I must get angry"

What might be some of the other names for the evaluation? There are elements of *blaming, accusing, finding fault, condemning* and *passing judgment,* followed by *justifying.*

These are what I call combination thoughts. They are large collections of individual upsetting thoughts, put together much like a computer macro, and it is programmed to "kick in" almost instantaneously when a certain stimulus or class of stimulus is perceived. So the first part of Tool #2 is to recognize the lightning fast sentences we tell ourselves between stimulus and response.

Write them down.

The train of thought may be longer than the example I gave above, and each component can act as a trigger for the whole macro. (A macro is a short, often-used program that other programs can call upon to perform a simple task such as calculating sales tax.)

Some of these statements we tell ourselves are exaggerations. Some are distortions and incorrect understandings, left over from childhood. Some are actually lies we tell ourselves.

The next step is to challenge the accuracy of these statements, accusations, judgments, and justifications. Challenge their truthfulness. Challenge whether or not they even apply.

Let us take another look at it.

STIMULUS			RESPONSE
PERCEPTION AND EVALUATION			
"That's horrible terrible awful"	"That shouldn't happen" to me	"Anybody would get angry"	"Therefore I must get angry"

CHALLENGE			
"Who says? maybe it's only frustrating, inconvenient, disappointing"	"Who says? Stuff happens Who should it happen to instead?"	"Who says? This is just exaggeration"	"Who says? Even if everybody" else would do I have to?"

Each one of the elements of combination thoughts is best dealt with one at a time.

For the next three weeks, we assign a new task to the Thought Monitor. That task is to identify combination thoughts, and to bring them to conscious awareness. These combination thoughts manifest as the "BIG UPSETS" and the "HOT BUTTONS" in your "Upset Response." It is important to NAME your Response accurately, as far as possible. Did you feel insulted? Or disrespected? Or shamed? Or pushed aside? Or belittled? Or treated un-fairly? Etc. This will assist you in organizing your thoughts when writing the EVALUATION portion above (which you will then CHALLENGE later).

Do not worry about the Thought Monitor's ability to handle this extra task, and continue to do the previous assignment of building the thought monitor with Tool #1.

Do take the time, at least, to make for yourself a brief note about the combination thought you identified, so you can dissect it at a convenient time if you cannot do this right away.

There will *not* be an hourly trigger for this task.

END OF WEEK ONE AFTER TOOL #2A

Most people are quite frustrated after the first week of Tool #2.

There seems to be so much more work to it than it first appeared. Every leaf turned over reveals another leaf, or a rock or a stick that demands to be dealt with. Cries of, "It's too hard," "I'm too embarrassed,? "Will I ever get through this one?" and, "It's so confusing," are some of the common statements.

Some have been so stressed, they lapsed on doing the Thought Monitor. That's the bad news.

The good news is, this is just a 'speed bump', and it gets easier quite quickly.

If you are distressed at this point - and many are - re-establish the Thought Monitor (Tool #1), and do so for a couple of days, while leaving Tool #2 alone. When you feel more peaceful, and want to begin again, re-read Tool #2, and begin to write out the diagram on a fresh piece of paper. This time focus on not skipping any thoughts, any steps, any justifications. When you write down an item, make sure you've written your *emotional response* to it, not just your judgment of the item that disturbs you.

Remember that this Big Upset is, in all likelihood, not new and may have plagued you for many years. You are not going to dissolve it overnight, but you are going to dissolve it for good!

This would be a good time to go to Appendix B (starts on page 68) and select a reading, perhaps "Stillness." Consider starting your day by reading "Stillness" for the next week, or maybe ending your day with it would work better for you.

END OF WEEK TWO AFTER TOOL #2A

If you are typical, you have conquered some of the challenges found in Tool #2A. Perhaps you begin to see why it is always recommended you apply a tool for at least three weeks, just to learn how to do it.

It is important to continue practicing the Thought Monitor until it is automatic, and no longer needs the trigger technique. Also continue to use Tool #2A whenever a 'big deal' rears its head. Remember, you don't have to deal with it in its entirety right at the moment it comes into your awareness, but it would be a good idea to jot down a few notes to yourself about it, and make an appointment with yourself for a specific time and place to deal with it later.

Sometime over the next week, go to Appendix B and read another article, perhaps the one on Forgiveness.

TOOL #2B
FACE-TO-FACE WITH SELF, MORE "CHALLENGE THE IDEA"

AN UN-DOING

In the previous section, we explored our upsetting feelings that seemed to result as the effect of an external stimulus. We saw that, in reality, we had created the upsetting result as a response to our perception of the external stimulus. We had felt attacked.

In this section, we will explore some of our own attacks.

STIMULUS   RESPONSE

Rather than the stimuli, let us look at some of our various responses: Sometimes we might want another to feel pain similar to what we felt; or we might want them to feel guilt or shame for a particular action; we might withhold love or attention in order to induce the fear of loss in them; we might want them to "see how it feels," "teach them a lesson" or punish them in some way. I will call these "stingers."

It is very rare for anybody to acknowledge initiating a primary attack. Almost always, our attacks are justified as responses, as counterattacks, while carefully holding the other responsible for stimulating our attack as we absolve ourselves of most, if not all, blame and guilt.

As always, the amount of time between stimulus and response seems to be zero. The sentences between stimulus and response are still full of blaming, accusing, finding fault, condemning, passing judgment, and finally justification.

If questioned about the delivery of one of the stingers, one can usually clearly point to a perceived stimulus ('something someone did to me') as justification. The stimulus *is* not the real justification. The sentences between the stimulus and response are within the mind of the one doing the "stinging."

Let us select now one of those "stinger/responses" that is in our repertoire and our memory banks. For example, "shame on you." Now select the stimulus that seemed to generate the response: "They didn't do a good job."

STIMULUS	STINGER/RESPONSE
"They didn't do a good job?	"Shame on them."

Now let's look at the EVALUATION. Remember, this is the part between Stimulus and Response.

This is shoddy work.	They are slacking on purpose	This reflects poorly on me	They are inferior.	I must shame them.

This train of judgment and justification now allows the response of the Stinger.

Now let's challenge these ideas:

Maybe so.	Who says? Maybe this is the best they have	Who says? Likely it reflects on them more	Who says? Maybe just an easy target	Who says? Is there a better way?

Evaluate one of your own "stingers" in this manner now, and another in three days, twice a week for three weeks. Use items from your past memory, and if a current opportunity arises, use that also.

Bear in mind that one of the ways we deliver "stingers" is without the other person knowing we're doing it. Examples are backbiting and gossip. These have the function of allowing us to feel superior or of belonging to an "in group" but have insidious effect of damaging another person's reputation and perhaps even their standing in the community. If you notice yourself being involved in this category, this would be a good time to challenge that idea as well.

TOOL #2C
RECOGNITION, WHEN TOOL #2A
MEETS TOOL #2B

AN UN-DOING

In Tool #2A, we see that one could respond by making oneself feel upset, or could remain at peace, depending on which thoughts and meanings one chooses to apply to their perception of the Stimulus.

In Tool #2B, we see that one may use their Response as a Stimulus to generate a Stinger if one chooses to, by using a series of thoughts and meanings to justify that.

In addition, we may see that in Tool #2A, the Stimulus that we perceive may be a Stinger delivered by someone else to you, to which you may respond by upsetting yourself.

The sequence for persons X and Y might look like this: X receives a Stimulus, and generates a Response/Stinger. Y receives that Response/Stinger as a Stimulus and upsets self. Y then might use that upset to justify generating a Stinger to send back to X.

As an alternative, either X or Y might 'challenge the idea,' and permanently interrupt the cycle.

"Recognition is a Law. What you Recognize will become quickened and active!"

—from *YOU* by Frances Wilshire.

When you Recognize a person, place or thing, you have the option to Recognize it as all the way "good" on the one hand, or all the way "not-good" on the other hand, or any mixture or degree in between.

When you Recognize the all "good" in a person, place or thing, you are Recognizing the "All Good or God Presence" within them, which calls forth the "good" into *active* manifestation. You resonate with the reality of the essential "good" of them. This enhances and activates the "good" not only in them, but in you, as well.

When you Recognize the "not-good" in a person, place or thing, you are Recognizing a "not-God Presence" within them, which calls forth the "not-good" into *active* manifestation. You then resonate with (agree with) the 'not-reality" or the "not-essence" of the other. The energy and vibration of both, then, tends to diminish.

In review:

One can Recognize the "good."

The other can Recognize the "good."

One can Recognize the "not-good."

The other can Recognize the "not-good."

Both can Recognize the "good,"' and thereby become *parters* in Recognition, and activate each other and their surroundings, to great benefit.

Both can Recognize the "not-good," and thereby become *partners* in Recognition, as enemies, but *partners,* nevertheless.

One can Recognize the "good," and the other can Recognize the "not-good," which either will prevent a partnership from forming, or dissolve one that had been formed.

The next time you are ready to CHALLENGE THE IDEA, put your challenge in the following way: "Am I Recognizing the 'good' or the 'not-good' with each sentence I am telling myself, and do I want to continue this PARTNERSHIP?"

PART FIVE
TOOL #3: PRINCIPLES AND IDEALS

AN UN-DOING

We all govern our lives by ideals and principles. The ideals and principles you choose are not likely to be exactly the same as those someone else has chosen. We choose *what* we choose because we believe those ideals and principles are consistent with the attainment of the highest good we are able to achieve.

Most people are unaware they actually have two main sets of ideals and principles. One set relates to your physical/material reality, and the other relates to your moral/religious/spiritual reality.

Since we are generally unaware of the two systems of thought, we tend to mix them together as though they are the same system, with variable degrees of success.

We will sort these two systems and demonstrate how each operates. Once this is done, you will be able to distinguish which one is being used in any circumstance, at any time.

In the *physical/material system* of reality, we strive to lay a foundation of the most important building blocks first.

The issue of HEALTH is very important to nearly everyone. We want to be healthy and to preserve our health. We might compromise our health on a short term basis, but we usually expect to get it back later. An example would be working so hard that you become exhausted, while relying on getting enough rest later to return you to health.

Having a HOME, whether you own it or not, is also an important consideration. This is even important to 'homeless' people, who will carry their 'home' with them, in the form of a bedroll and a few possessions.

FAMILY is important, whether it is a biological family, a non-biological family such as group living situation, or a tribal environment such as belonging to a branch of the military or a religious community. Some people will settle for just one other significant person or even a pet to fill this category.

FINANCE is the next basic building block in this system of the physical/ material set of ideals. This represents the ability to exchange things of value. This can be in the form of money, trading or bartering goods, or the exchange of effort or services.

These four represent the foundation of our physical/ material endeavors, and will generally be maintained. The next steps will not be taken without them.

The next steps usually include *accumulating additional possessions,* finding a *mate,* and having *children,* This is followed by a period of time for consolidation, enhancing the living space, and providing more desirable items or circumstances for yourself, your mate, and your children.

Following this period of consolidation, steps are generally taken to improve *status* in whatever community you find yourself, and eventually you will strive to find a *special niche* to fill that is unique. This can be a career, a vocation or a core passion. Art, business or counseling are examples of this.

The final goal is to reach that which you have defined as *success,* while preserving the building blocks that support it.

This can be thought of as *having* enough.

HAVING ENOUGH

SUCCESS

CAREERS   STATUS

POSSESSIONS   MATE   CHILDREN

HEALTH   HOME   FAMILY/TRIBE   FINANCE

In this system of physical/ material thought, the focus tends to be on the external world rather than the internal world of attitudes and emotions.

Therefore, only big issues of upset receive attention, while 'little' hurts, upsets, angers, and so forth, tend to be buried, discounted, or ignored because they seem to not affect the big picture.

If the 'little' upsets are repetitive and accumulate, however, or are combined with other upsets, they can become a big issue and will be dealt with, usually by a change in external behavior. This is particularly true if they threaten any of the structural building blocks.

Notice that the bottom row of building blocks, in a very real sense, control the upper rows. You will generally only go 'up' to the next level if you are certain it will not jeopardize the level on which you stand. For example, you may be about to land a major new client when a health crisis in the family puts that on hold.

The *moral / religious / spiritual system,* the system of ideals and principles, operates differently in several ways. In this system, your focus is primarily on internal development, from which your external behaviors proceed automatically. In this system, all of the ideals and principles are interchangeable, and one is not higher or better than another. However, this *level* of moral

/ religious / spiritual thought tends to control the thoughts and actions on the physical/ material *system or level* of thought.

In this system, every 'little' upsetting thought is important because it interferes with internal development of precisely the ideal or principle governing that situation at that moment.

In this system, the goal is *being* enough rather than *having* enough.

BEING ENOUGH

REUNION WITH GOD-LOVE

REALIZATION OF ONENESS WITH ALL

UNCONDITIONAL LOVE   SPIRITUAL SELFISHNESS

AWARENESS WISDOM GENEROSITY ENLIGHTENMENT

INTEGRITY HONESTY SPIRITUALITY FORGIVENESS
LETTING GO

KINDNESS COMPASSION EMPATHY HARMONY
TEACHING

FAITH UNDERSTANDING PURITY OF FOCUS TRUTH

HEALING PEACE SERVICE FREEDOM JOYFUL

PATIENCE TOLERANCE FAITHFULNESS

OPEN-MINDEDNESS

Now, the first task of building the Thought Monitor is firmly becoming habit. If this is *not* true for you yet, continue your focus on Tool #1 before starting this tool, Tool #3.

Tool #2 is closely related to Tool #1 and will tend to be automatically active as you focus on Tool #1.

The task for Tool #3 is to once again to build in a trigger to be activated about once an hour to identify a random thought, and to ask a single question:

"Which system of ideals and principles does this thought represent? The physical/ material world, or the moral/religious/ spiritual world?"

Just by asking the question, the focus may shift without effort. There is no correct or incorrect focus here, because both parts are needed in this world to some extent.

The purpose here is to develop an *awareness* of your thoughts, and systems, of ideals and principles, not to fix them. As the habit develops and you become more aware, the proportion of thoughts in each system will shift and adjust almost automatically to be appropriate to your current level of development at the time.

Three weeks of hourly monitoring, while awake, is the assignment. You will find the Noticer/Watcher/Observer can easily perform this function while you are still performing the functions of the first two tools.

END OF WEEK ONE AFTER TOOL #3

During this past week, most people find issues of a spiritual or religious nature coming to the forefront. We find it inevitable that students' spiritual nature becomes part of the mix at this juncture, as the focus, for the time being, on only those concepts of a purely spiritual nature rather than those of 'brand name' religions.

Many of these thoughts will be upsetting, Do not try to 'fix' them. Remember, the goal is to become aware.

Some students find they are aware of *more* than just the two sets of Principles and Ideals. In fact, they may discover several sub-sets within themselves.

Go to Appendix C (starts on page 75) for articles to read each week related to the topic presented here.

PART SIX
TOOL #4: THE THREE O's

AN UN-DOING

Sometimes things seem overwhelming because they appear so complex. Much of this complexity is an illusion invented by the same process that cost us most of our free will. The reality is much simpler.

This can be illustrated by the three O's.

1) OBSERVATIONS

Observations are about those things that *are*. The world is round. Much of the world's surface is water. Some land is flat while other land is hilly. Some is covered with vegetation while another part is desert. Observations are generally accepted as fact and not subject to active control.

2) OCCURRENCES

Occurrences make up the majority on which our attention is focused. These are events of everyday life. Storms happen, things break, people get sick or well, items get lost or found, items get stolen, we are lied to or cheated, target goals are met or not met, we win or lose, and people make mistakes, to name a few of the occurrences we might perceive. Occurrences are generally regarded as variable and subject to someone's control.

3) OMISSIONS

Omissions are events that are anticipated but do not happen. They include appointments not kept, mail not delivered, love not received, and promises not fulfilled. It might also be a traffic ticket you deserved but did not receive, and even intentional omissions, such as choosing not to do what you promised.

OBSERVATIONS, OCCURRENCES, AND OMISSIONS

There are two ways to react to these:

A) You can put meaning on them;

B) Or not.

If you put meaning on them, you will be upset. This is true even if you believe you are only selecting a positive meaning. For example, suppose you decide to purchase an item of clothing. You select it for color, style, fit, material, and quality of workmanship. You are pleased with your purchase because of all the positive qualities it has. You have placed *positive* meaning on it.

Most people are unaware they also, subconsciously or unconsciously, program into themselves, the criteria for being upset. You could now tell me instantly, without even thinking about it, what meaning you would put on it if that item of clothing were to become lost, stolen, damaged, torn, stained, or the seams failed. This is because *positive* is the flip-side of *negative*. When you evaluated the positive attributes of the item of clothing, you did so in terms of the absence of negative attributes. You selected the 'right' style from a mental list of styles, many of which were 'wrong.' You chose the 'right' fit from a mental list of the many possibilities in which the fit would be 'wrong.' And the right color from a mental list of colors in which many of the colors would be 'wrong.'

You identified with your selection and said to yourself, in effect, "This is consistent with me and with how I see myself and with how I want to present myself to the external world." You put meaning on the item of clothing. You agreed to those criteria by which you would decide to feel 'good.' Ahead of time, you also agreed to and reinforced those criteria by which you would decide to feel 'bad.' You also reinforced previous 'bad' feelings from related events in the past.

If you decide not to put meaning on Observations, Occurrences, or Omissions, you allow yourself to stay at peace, experience joy, and feel love.

OBSERVATIONS, OCCURRENCES, and OMISSIONS do not have any meaning of their own. They are just facts. A hundred people could perceive the same occurrence and none would put on a meaning identical to that of any other single person. The meanings are arbitrary and are an invention of the person supplying the meaning. If you are at peace, you may stay there by refusing to give meaning to the meaningless.

If you are not at peace, you may regain peace by withdrawing the meaning you gave to the meaningless. This is true about whatever circumstance occupies your mind at any time.

Over the next three weeks, add this task to your Thought Monitor: after you have evaluated a random thought as upsetting, recognize it is meaningless except for the meaning you gave it. You do not need to 'fix' the meaning, find the 'right' meaning, or anything else in this endeavor other than developing awareness.

PART SEVEN
Tool #5: MEANING AND PURPOSE, AND BEHAVIOR

Any event, when viewed by more than one person, will usually receive a meaning from each. They will not be identical, and may not even be close to identical. The availability of all options for meaning, and the desire of each person to be unique and to have a unique perspective, will make it so.

Each will evaluate, usually in lightning quick fashion, the options for meaning, from all the way good on the one hand, to all the way bad on the other, and choose the one they want from somewhere in between.

It is estimated there are six billion people in the world, and with the current state of communication, there have been events that the majority of the world has become aware of during the time the event was taking place, and each one placed his own unique meaning on the event. No two were exactly the same.

Then, discussion began about whose meaning was the correct one, or whose was the most accurate. Depending on the intensity of the discussion and the stage of the 'development of the meaning,' an individual may alter his or her perception of the meaning, week to week, day to day, hour to hour, or even minute to minute.

Man searches externally, time after time after time, and asks, "What is the meaning of this or that or the other thing?" and may ultimately ask, "What is the meaning of the world?" This is a foundational question, which we will call Foundational Question #1.

Likewise, when any event occurs, if it is significant enough, attempts at understanding the event often involve the exploration of what the event is for, or how can it be utilized, how should it be valued, or what is its purpose, chosen from a long list of possible purposes. Ultimately, one may ask, "What is the purpose of the world?" This is also a foundational question, which we will call Foundational Question #2.

We seem to be evaluating possible answers to these questions at all times at some level, and are responding to these possible answers by constantly adjusting our behavior in order to be more aligned with our momentary perception of 'reality.' We test out all sorts of strategies and behaviors, and in the process, try to decide what we want and what we do not want.

We want to establish which would be our best form of behavior for each situation. We might even ask, "What would be the best basis for my behavior?" This we will call Foundational Question #3.

Since Foundational Questions #1 & #2 have not been answered adequately, and indeed, the answers we do have keep changing, the basis for our behavior in Foundational Question #3 seems to be aimed at a moving target, as well.

It seems safer to use the rules laid down by others, rather than trusting ourselves to generate our own rules.

We have looked at an ever changing landscape in our view of the world for answers to Foundational Questions #1, #2, and #3, and we wanted the answers to have stability. We have been disappointed.

Are there any answers in the spiritual realm that have relevance? Consider these thoughts.

For Foundational Question #1- "What is the Meaning of the world?" - we look at the world as a place of matter, and its events as events of matter. We also tend to look at the events of matter in terms of their effect on the world and its occupants. We search for answers from each other, from nature, and from science. When we seek externally in this way for answers to these questions, we usually formulate the questions in such a way, and expect answers in such a way, that they support the primacy of the body more often than the primacy of the spirit.

We neglect to consider that the Builder and Architect may have supplied the meaning right from the beginning. If that is so, all the meanings we have put on the world since then, in so far as they are apart from the Builder's, are meaningless!

The world either had meaning from the beginning, or it must be meaningless now.

If the world had meaning from the beginning, what might it be? The Parent made something wonderful, for example, a world or a universe, and gave it to the Child to experience. Something made out of Love, given to the Object of Love, the Child. The MEANING OF THE WORLD, then, is Love, right from the beginning, in every one of its aspects, including you. Not as people in general see love, but as you now do.

For Foundational Question #2 - "What is the Purpose of the world?" - the answer to this question also relates to the Child, who went into the world to experience the world.

The Child went into the world, made some mistakes, became confused, lost its way, and felt guilty (i.e., tried to figure things out by putting meaning on them).

This created the need to correct the mistakes, reverse the confusion, and dissolve the guilt. This is called *forgiveness*. The PURPOSE OF THE WORLD, then, is to provide an arena for the Child to have experiences and to forgive the errors of the Child.

These answers to Foundational Questions #1 & #2 are solid

and resist change because they are conceptual rather than specific, yet can be applied to each specific. These form a basis for the answer to Foundational Question #3, which deals with *behavior.*

The behavior itself is not so important. One might still identify self as a salesperson, doctor, or a laborer. Variations within that frame are likely to occur if the answer to Foundational Questions #1 and #2 are chosen as ideals.

If, indeed, you accept that the meaning of the world is love, and the world includes you, you tend then, to become the meaning. You tend to behave as love behaves, and you tend to *be* love. Trust yourself to be conscientious and responsible and caring.

If you accept you are here to experience rather than just to endure, then choose to become a person who experiences, trusting yourself to be conscientious, responsible and caring. If you accept you are here to forgive, then choose to become forgiveness, or the expression of that quality, especially toward self, trusting yourself to be conscientious, responsible and caring, and without being a pushover.

One might choose to focus on a different aspect of forgiveness such as peace, love, or joy, for their ideal, and these are good places to begin, also. It is well to be active in the application of these as ideals, and ask at any given moment 'of the choices presented to me, which are the more helpful to living *my* ideals?' Let that answer be the guide to your behavior rather than being guided by the rules someone else imposed upon you.

Now that you *own* the Meaning and Purpose you have chosen, gradually begin to do whatever you want, choosing your way, trusting yourself to be conscientious and responsible and caring.

Remember the title of this course? You are now more free. You are now free to do, have freedom from, and are free to be. To activate this freedom, you must now do the choosing, rather than using someone else's choice for you. Now the foundational questions have been answered and will not change.

How might this be incorporated into the Thought Monitor? Now your Thought Monitor has begun functioning on a somewhat regular basis, and a great many troublesome thoughts are leaving, it would be good to have something to put in their place.

Examples might be:

"I could see peace instead of this."

"I remember (a specific) joy instead." "The meaning of the world is Love." "I forgive myself."

"I choose the most helpful thought." "My purpose is forgiveness."

Put some form of this function into your Thought Monitor, and it will reinforce the gains you have made and those you will continue to make. To make it most helpful, commit to regular practice, similar to previous practices.

THE ULTIMATE TOOL

This Tool will only release its full realization insofar as the other Tools have become fully integrated into one's being.

The ultimate tool is a decision.

It is a decision to use the body and human activity for the purpose of growth and development of the talents, skills and strengths of the spirit, and to enlist the ego and the physical in support of that.

This does not mean withdrawing from material life: rather it means being more involved in the awareness of the activities of the material and physical life, and a focus of purpose and intent that all activity be consistent with the maintaining and furthering an environment of enhancing the highest and best of the spiritual.

Rather than make the physical, the body, and material activities your enemy, make the body and its ego important servants in the activity of nurturing and maturing known and latent talents of spirit, the most universal of which is *intuition.*

It is this talent of intuition that allows you to know when it is appropriate and wise to *comfort* another in need of comfort.

The most universally recognized talent of spirit, also called a 'gift of spirit,' is that of *healing.* This can be done on many levels, from the kissing of a child's bruised finger, to the physician's prayer asking for guidance to choose the correct treatment, to miraculous instantaneous healing through spirit.

To *bless* means to make holy, to spiritualize, to sanctify, and to Recognize the God-part of a person, place, thing, or situation, thereby activating it toward its highest potential.

To *heal,* to *comfort* and to *bless,* are activities the body may be used for. If the focus is limited to these three, then the body and the ego *are* in the service of the higher, or spiritual, self. Develop these as a habit, commit to these as a way of living, accessing the skills you have gained, through the process of developing the Thought Monitor. Then these are yours: peace, love, harmony, healing, joy, decisiveness, and more.

EPILOGUE

LET'S PRETEND

In the beginning, someone may have asked a question such as, "Is there anything of meaning besides the completeness of what God gives? And it is as though God answered, "Go check it out. Check out every way you can think of."

So we played a game of LET'S PRETEND. Let's pretend the next new thing or circumstance will give something that God doesn't. In every new experience we approached, we agreed to anticipate that this just might be the one with the meaning and fulfillment that has been missing. Individually and collectively, we have searched every corner of the world and even are beginning to explore outside our world, and have explored in every way we have been able to think of, so far.

We have been doing that forever, and when we are satisfied that the dichotomies of win/lose, poverty/wealth, success/failure, war/peace, and all the others are not the places where some new meaning is hiding, then those pursuits will cease to distract us.

Then we will be more open to original joy, original peace, and original love.

A NEXT STEP

In general, each person in this world receives a thorough education in awareness of the body, and of the physical, material aspects of the world around them. Each has formed ideas concerning the uses and misuses of the things, circumstances and relationships they encounter on a regular basis.

Each has also formed some understanding of what is called the mind or mental activities, yet that understanding is generally more limited than the understanding each has of the body and the material.

The discipline we might bring into our life, while mental in origin, is more often focused upon the body, while discipline as to what quality of thoughts we will allow in the mind or mental environment is lacking.

There are two distinct elements of mind: (1) sequential thought, evaluative in nature, and quite prominent and noisy; (2) awareness, not sequential, and very quiet.

This latter, quiet aspect is most often drowned out and covered up, and paid little attention to by most people. Yet, it is this aspect that people really seek when they are seeking after those 'quality of life' issues, but seeking them externally rather than first going internally.

This course, A REDISCOVERY OF FREE WILL, is a course in awareness and ownership of the mind and mental activities to a greater degree (for it cannot be done in an absolute manner in a physical body). It is preparatory to, and introductory to, subsequent curricula dealing with the development of awareness of the spirit part of self, and the growth, development, maturation, and strengthening of the individual's spiritual abilities.

APPENDIX A

REVERSE UN-PRODUCTIVE THINKING

Most truths are simple yet profound, and can be delivered in few pages or less. Each of the following 'tools' is a simple yet profound concept. Putting them into practice is simpler than most people make them, but not necessarily easy, depending on the individual's barriers to the learning. These principles and ideas foster self-improvement and can be applied equally well to business, hobbies, sports, parenting, leisure, or spiritual development. For maximum benefit, each should be practiced for at least three weeks, both to give a fair trial, and to decide whether you want to integrate it into your life at the current time. INVEST IN YOURSELF WITH TIME, ENERGY AND FOCUS.

YOU ARE ALREADY PERFECT AND I CAN PROVE IT!

Perfection seems to be a big deal. Most people continually try to do something better, so called 'self-improvement programs' that usually deal with performance, getting a better score on a test, getting a better job, perfecting a technique and so forth. We talk about perfecting ourselves and reaching some goal and idealizing the goal, so when we get there, it will be just perfect. And, of course, when we get there, there is a new goal, or a new vision of perfection and it never seems enough.

So how on earth do we reach perfection, how do we become perfect? It seems to be an eternal quest for human beings.

Well, the issue is, you are already perfect. Does that seem like a contradiction? Well, not really.

The problem we seem to have is, we confuse doing perfectly

with being perfect. You already are perfect, and I will prove it.

Let's start with this idea to consider. In order to understand you are perfect, you must also understand you are innocent. That does not mean I think you are naive; you may or may not be, but that is a separate issue. You are innocent, no matter how many different ways you have tried to convince yourself you are guilty. I have heard people exclaim, "I know I am guilty," then argue with me vociferously that they are guilty and hang on to their guilt as though giving up their guilt will somehow be giving up their identity. Well, you are not guilty.

Consider this fact: In every circumstance you have found yourself in throughout your life, you have evaluated the circumstance as to its relative merits, its desirability or undesirability, its goodness or badness, its benefits and pitfalls. And when it came time to make the decision, you made the best possible decision you could at the time with the information you had to work with. Furthermore, you made whatever decision you did for the Good in it. Now it is easy today to use today's information to pass judgment on yesterday's events, and say they were wrong. It was not the best possible decision, but isn't there something inherently unfair about using today's information to pass judgment on yesterday's events? When you say, "I should have done this or that," so what? The greatest minds in history could have made better decisions if they could have used the information available to them in their tomorrows, but it wasn't. You made the best possible decision you could at the time with the information you had to work with, and you made it for the Good in it. In fact, I would be willing to bet you have never, ever, ever made a decision to do anything for the evil in it.

Yes, you may have acknowledged there was something undesirable in it, but at the time you made the decision, the trade-off seemed to make it worth it. You made it for the Good in it and you put up with whatever was not Good in order to get the Good.

Now would you expect anything more than that from anybody around you? Look around you. In anybody you advised, in anybody you talked to, you would tell them each and every time, "Make the best possible decision you can with the information you have to work with."

Clearly sometimes we have to make decisions with less than perfect information. But it isn't the information that makes us perfect. If we had perfect information, it would be a lot easier to make perfect decisions and turn in perfect performances, but even if we did make perfect performances, it would have nothing to do with guilt or innocence, would it?

So what is guilt? Self-blame. Since you already have seen you have made the best possible decision every time in your entire life with the information you had to work with, what kind of giant, morbid, egotistical trick is it to insist that, using the resources available to you at the time, you should be guilty because you fell short of some artificial performance mark?

It would be good for you to give up the guilt and acknowledge one more item of information. Since you are a unique individual, you will never, ever be able to perform perfectly according to somebody else's standards. You cannot reach perfection that way. Since you are a unique individual, and since you are reading this, you are not dead yet, you have more decisions to make. Whose standards are you going to apply? It would probably be best *being our* standards. You are here to learn and grow, and in your life, there is nobody in the entire universe more perfectly suited than you to do the next thing you must do, and to make the next decision you must make. You are perfectly suited to do the role you call your life.

Will your performance be flawed? If so, according to whose standards? Someone else's? Do not confuse performance with perfection; you are already perfect, you are just not finished yet!

Let me give you a performance example. It doesn't matter whether your performances are *big* or small, whether you are creating a masterpiece in the kitchen, carving a piece of wood, manufacturing an automobile, or whatever it is you do. It takes some time, some effort, and the goal is often to do it and do it well. Without a flaw. Perfectly. So suppose you do this thing of yours and it comes out perfectly. Now, when it was half-way done, was it perfect?

Of course it was perfect. It had to be perfect, at half-way. If *it* was not perfect at half-way, it would not be perfect when it was done. At half-way, it was merely not completed yet, but it was perfectly suited to being completed perfectly. You are like that project - incomplete, not done yet. But just being 'not done yet' does not mean you are not perfect. You are.

May you have the courage to go forward responsibly and conscientiously, guiltless, therefore innocent, acknowledging your own inner perfection.

HONESTY, DISCLOSURE AND TRUTH

These three terms are, at times, used interchangeably. Honesty and Truth are both emotionally charged for many people compared to Disclosure.

Both Honesty and Truth, for instance, have been described in terms of telling a lie. Truth has also been described as referring to a concept of reality that does not change, such as the Law of Gravity. Truth has also been described as a concept that depicts the opposite of false, where false is not a lie, but merely an error. For example, four centuries ago, Church leaders maintained the truth that the Sun orbits the Earth. They were honest in that truth, even though it later proved erroneous.

Both Truth and Honesty have been applied in situations

where accuracy and inaccuracy are at issue. Examples are 'honest scales' and 'truth in lending.'

Disclosure and Honesty are often juxtaposed when you insist another be forthcoming with what is on their mind, and the interrogator might say, "Come on now, be honest," or if Truth be the hammer, "Come on now, tell the truth." This is a form of pressure upon the right to not disclose whatever the one would prefer not to say.

Disclosure, then, is to make external that which is internal, or to 'say what is on your mind.'

Truth is more variable in its definitions, from confessing a wrongdoing, to telling what you know with as much accuracy and detail as you are able, to the discovery and iteration of some hypothetical absolute truth. Meanwhile honesty, while many would doubtless insist it conform to sets of externally imposed regulations, remains at its core, an internal process. It may or may not have anything to do with either Truth or Disclosure.

Honesty merely means that nothing you do, say or omit, contradicts anything you think. Conversely, it also means everything you do, say or omit, matches what you think. Therefore, you may think in error (not the truth) and still be honest in terms of doing, saying and omitting. Also, you may think in error (or in truth, for that matter), and still have the right to a separate choice as to whether or not to Disclose.

Therefore, Honesty does not mean Truth, nor Disclosure. Truth does not mean Honesty, nor Disclosure. Disclosure does not mean Honesty, nor Truth.

Yet, under certain circumstances, all might be present.

TRUST

In our natural state, we trust.

It is clear shortly after birth that there is a drive to trust.

It is clear, dis-trusting and mis-trusting are learned behaviors. These are distortions of trust and misuse or mis-applications of trust.

Notice I did not say, 'not trusting.'

Trust is an energy that accompanies us, part of our basic essence, and we have to put it somewhere, use it somehow, but we all seem to have an abundance of it.

When we dis-trust or mis-trust, we distort or misplace the natural drive to trust that the universe is unfolding as it should, that we are a legitimate part of it, and instead trust something else.

We put our trust in the notion, "'They' are out to get us," and adjust our behavior accordingly. We trust dichotomies, by putting meanings on virtually everything we perceive, those of good and bad, tall and short, better and worse, speaking well or poorly, dressing appropriately or inappropriately, winning and losing, and countless others. We trust that change is inevitable and we can only rely on ourselves, because everyone else is more unreliable than we are. We trust the truth of 'no pain, no gain,' and 'the price of any success is a certain amount of suffering.' We trust in the notion, "Anything that can go wrong will go wrong." And most of all, we trust that the meaning we as individuals put on anything is the correct one and, if this meaning changes, we will correctly put the new meaning in place. And we trust, if we are shown to be wrong, it is because nobody can be right all of the time.

We put our trust in the material, the worldly, the people, the money, the circumstances, the events, the experiences. We trust anything at all, except that things will work out as they are supposed to.

Your task: Once each hour, while awake, is to notice your thoughts, and ask yourself, "Where am I placing my trust, right now?"

APPENDIX B

By this time, the Thought Monitor function, initially given into the keeping of the "Watcher, Noticer, Observer" part of self, has likely encountered some sabotage, as the ego part of self has tried to take over this function for lower-self purposes.

If this has occurred, re-read Tool #1, and re-establish the conscious connection with the Noticer (my favorite designation for this function. Watcher and Observer are equally as valid). Re-enforce this connection often.

STILLNESS

When we want to meditate or pray, we typically try to create an inner space of quietness, silence, or stillness.

Many methods and techniques have evolved and have been used throughout time to accomplish this.

Usually, we will control the external environment by going to a quiet place, or entering into a quiet enclosure, or removing any distracting or noise-producing things, people or animals.

Paradoxically, we may then add stimuli, such as music, various smells such as incense or sage, lights or candles, or ingest substances in order to try to make the body more receptive.

When all this is in readiness, we turn to the inner and begin to focus the mind, perhaps on chants or other sounds, or we may focus on lights, or even on an idea, in pursuit of getting to the STILLNESS.

The good news is, those who put forth this effort to achieve the STILLNESS usually do achieve it, and are rewarded with experiences that leave them with lasting, and often life-transforming, impressions. Still, these concepts that have been handed down to us from times past are saturated with a sense of mysteriousness and strangeness, of special-ness and initiation, and of worthiness beyond the reach of the average person. And that is just the good stuff. The references to the pitfalls of the darker applications of seeking the STILLNESS would make one think noise is a blessed event.

Are you conscientious and responsible? Are you cautious yet caring? Do you trust yourself to continue with these qualities? Can you, plus God, handle anything that comes your way? If your answers are "Yes," then I invite you to the STILLNESS, and I invite you to it the easy way.

STILLNESS is *normal.* It is with you all the time! It is the noise that is not normal. STILLNESS will remain once you get rid of all the noise. You don't have to 'go' anywhere, ingest anything, light any candles, recite any chants, say foreign words, or pass any tests or initiations to claim your right to your STILL-NESS. There are no 'magic' formulas.

Yet, you might want to use some of these things as tools to help you focus. There is nothing special about the tools. And the tool you might choose may not be one that would work for anyone else. The *user* of the tool is the achiever, the tool does not achieve.

When you want to experience the STILLNESS, just realize you are already in the STILLNESS. Then gently push away and dismiss any distraction, any clutter or clatter from your mind, and focus on removing those, rather than striving for the STILLNESS. The STILLNESS is not going anywhere; you cannot lose it. It is what is left, as part of your essence, when everything that hides it from your awareness has lost its ability to command your attention.

It is normal to have times of STILLNESS. It is your birth-right. Be normal. Claim your birthright.

NATURE OF FORGIVENESS

Few people understand the nature of forgiveness, and fewer still understand the nature of the conditions that set up the need for forgiveness.

The world teaches you, if you say you are sorry, acknowledge your mistake and promise to make efforts not to repeat the mistake, you may be forgiven. There may or may not be an associated punishment involved. Either way, with those who elect themselves to watch over such things, whether they be parents, teachers, employers, or a governmental agency, there is almost always an element of observation to see whether or not you make the same mistake again, with the implied promise that if you do, you are then at risk for a punishment or more punishment. In a situation like this, you don't feel totally forgiven and you don't feel the slate is ever wiped clean.

In order to understand better how forgiveness gets that way, one must understand what kinds of things set up the need for forgiveness. Usually this happens as follows: First there is some sort of event or stimulus. The person sees the stimulus, spends a short amount of time perceiving it, and that leads to upset. This indeed is the way it occurs, but what most people don't realize is that the processing step is the second step. It is not a bang/bang, stimulus/upset, kind of thing. What really happens is, the stimulus creates a series of sentences inside a person's head. They happen fast, and so automatically that we are not aware of them, but as I point them out to you, you will recognize them. So when the stimulus happens and you perceive it, there follows a first sentence that says something like, "This is horrible, this is terrible, this is awful."

This leads to another sentence perhaps, "This shouldn't happen to me," which leads to the next conclusion, "Anybody who had this happen would get upset." The next step is, "Therefore,

I must get upset." And lo and *behold, you have upset!*

Do you recognize this process? I have a name for this process, in fact I have several names for this process. It can be called Blaming, Accusing, Condemning, Finding Fault, Justifying, and, perhaps, Passing Judgment is the most appropriate name. Now you can see, the very first foundation for setting up a situation that requires forgiveness is that you have passed judgment.

Is the judgment justified? Well, people have a tendency to always be able to justify their passing of judgment. I would like to point out, however, that almost everybody has experienced the situation in which they thought they understood a situation clearly and passed judgment on it, only to later find out they had incorrect information. It wasn't nearly as bad as they thought, but they still had the upset, even though the situation as they perceived it did not exist. So the upset-ness didn't even depend on whether the situation was true or not, or real or not; it only depended on the judging.

The same can be said for the opposite, in which you have experienced a situation you thought was wonderful, only to find out later it wasn't wonderful. If you had known all of the facts, you would have judged it and been upset, but you didn't do it correctly. You missed out on being upset and had to postpone it until sometime later. So not only did the upset-ness not depend on the circumstances, but the feeling of wonderful did not depend on the circumstances either.

The reason I bring up these two hypothetical situations is to stimulate you to think about the possibility that some of your past upsets may have been in error, and that you are currently holding on to some of those upsets needlessly. You might say you don't want to judge anymore. You have clearly seen, contrary to popular opinion, God has not left the judgment seat empty so you could be the one to fill it while he went on vacation. Perhaps there are numerous times in which you did not have enough information to be passing judgment.

So then, you ask, "Well, what will I do about it?" "How do I change what has already gone before?" The best way I know is to first get it clearly in your mind what the steps were that led you to passing the judgment, and then to challenge them. In the first place, was it really 'horrible, terrible and awful'? Or was it merely inconvenient, frustrating and disappointing?

How about, "This should not happen to me"? Who should it have happened to? Or, "Anybody who had this happen to them would get upset"? That is probably not true; not everybody in the whole world would look at it that way, as you continue to challenge the idea. And finally, even if 'everybody else in the whole world would get upset,' why does that mean you have to?

Now I recommend you look at a few minor cases. No doubt you have a big one somewhere in your memory you would like to attack, but it is better to get practice on the little ones, and challenge them.

So what shall we call this process of re-thinking the original judgment, challenging it and perhaps dissolving some of the intensity, horribleness of whatever it was that stimulated, that caused, whatever kind of upset happened, and getting to the point where judgment is either dissolved or less severe?

If it is completely dissolved, then that's what I call Forgiveness. Then you will see, once you apply the challenge, and if you apply it successfully, the judgment will disappear and very quickly after that, forgiveness will disappear, too. They will both just sort of vanish in terms of their importance, but you will remember the experience to apply it next time.

There are two very important questions I have to ask you right now. In the examples above:

1. What gets forgiven?

2. Who gets forgiven?

You see, there isn't anything in the entire world that is so good you can't think about it in such a way you could find fault with it and see something bad about it. On the other hand, there is nothing in the world so bad you can't imagine some way that some good would come out of it. Therefore, you can think all the way in either direction about anything you see. Your thoughts about it are totally arbitrary. This is why you don't think the same way about anything exactly as anybody else in the world thinks about that same thing. When we look at the various stimuli we see in the world, we see them according to our own agenda. We have decided some way or another in our upbringing (the way that you were programmed) to respond to certain stimuli, in certain ways. Your total package is unique, and your response to the world you see is nobody else's response. Now you didn't exactly invent your response, since a lot of other people had a lot to do with programming you, but the way you are today and the way you respond today is the way, on some level, you have agreed to respond. When you were a child, you didn't have much choice about how you became programmed. However, if you wish to become aware, you can cast out how you have been programmed, deciding to see which of it you like and which you don't like. As a young adult, almost everybody decides there is part of their program they don't like, and chooses to change it, or replace it, or modify it in some way. In other words, they change their mind. There are some parts of the program people decide they are *not* going to change their mind about. They have passed judgment and they won't change their mind. This then becomes the major obstacle to forgiveness.

Did you answer the questions above?

Ultimately, the 'What' that gets forgiven is the thought with which we passed judgment.

The 'Who' that gets forgiven is the self, the thinker of the judgmental thought.

Everything that sets up the need for forgiveness occurs at the thought level.

Everything that dissolves the need for forgiveness occurs at the thought level.

Only the punishment, or lack of it, occurs on the material level.

APPENDIX C

SPIRITUAL SELFISHNESS

In a very special way, a person who is involved in the spiritual realm must always be selfish. For the truly spiritual person, the concept of unselfishness does not have much meaning.

Let me explain. While the world will teach you, if you give something away, you do not have it anymore, the spirit teaches you, if you give something away that's worth any spiritual value, you automatically have *more* of it after giving it away than you had before you gave it away. At the very least, you totally keep it, and yet still give it away.

Does this seem a contradiction?

A good example would be teaching. When you teach somebody, you give somebody new knowledge. It is knowledge you previously had. Not only do you keep that knowledge, but by the very act of teaching - which is a different perspective from learning- you often understand it better in the process of teaching than you did before you taught it.

So you can see why spiritual teachers will take every opportunity to give away what they have learned.

In the same way, those who are involved in spirituality will put relatively far less value on those things they can give away and appear not to keep, such as money. They would be more delighted to dispense pearls of wisdom than pearls from an oyster in the same way. Since spiritual teachers are most often also spiritual learners, they would take much more delight in receiving pearls of wisdom rather than pearls from an oyster. When they receive a spiritual 'nugget' of truth and are spiritually aware, they know instantly what to do with it. They will share it as soon as possible with somebody else they perceive can benefit from it. Whereas if they received a gold nugget of considerable worldly value, they will become distracted. For then they must try to decide what to do with it, where to place it, whether or not to display it, whether or not to insure it, and how to keep other people from taking it away from them.

Those who feast on spiritual truth want none of that. Does that mean they have no interest or need for physical materialistic goods and sustenance? By no means, it just means they have no use in general for a lot of extra amounts, or values that will distract them from their real interest.

They will want to grow in their own spiritual understanding, and be an opportunity for other people to grow in theirs.

Selfishly realizing that, as they elevate their own understanding, they elevate their own spiritual energy, and help others do the same. That is good for us, for all of us. What improves one improves the whole, and since they firmly understand they are part of the whole, whatever elevates somebody else, elevates them, and they very selfishly want that.

Obviously this selfishness is in service of the higher self, and assumes an understanding that we are all in it together and produces a win/win situation, rather than the selfishness in service of the lower self, which has the concept, "We are separate and what is good for me can be bad for you," and vice versa. In other words, a win/lose situation.

There are no unselfish acts or thoughts. We are either self-interested in service of the higher self, or self-interested in service of lower self.

For example, in war, imagine there are ten people in a fox hole into which a grenade falls, and one solider throws himself upon it. Is this because he wants to die? Typically not, although there may be exceptions. Generally, he recognizes there is an 'us,' and it is better for 'us' to have nine people alive than all ten dead. How do we know this? Sometimes there have been such heroic acts and the person has lived to tell about it because the grenade was a dud.

Therefore, always acknowledge your selfishness, and always seek to come to the awareness of whether or not your selfishness is in service of the higher self, or in terms of the lower self.

HEALING IS NOT ABOUT HEALING

How, then, should I approach the activity known as 'healing'? Healing of any sort will not take place unless there is receptivity, or a tendency toward receptivity in the individual to be healed, in any or all, of the 'mind,' the 'heart,' the 'soul,' the 'etheric body,' the 'emotional body,' the 'physical body.'

Generally, healing of the 'body' will not take place unless there is some change of the 'mind' or 'heart.' To the extent the 'mind' or 'heart' changes, the 'mind' or 'heart' will be healed to a corresponding extent. The 'body,' then, may or may not be healed, but usually is at least improved. This seems necessary for most people as an outward sign of inner healing.

The healing of the 'mind' or 'heart' is primary, and the healing of the 'body' is secondary.

Willingness, no matter how small, to change the 'inner,' on the part of the individual to be healed, or, if they do not have reasoning, on the part of their care-giver, is a pre-requisite.

What change of the 'inner' is necessary?

Only the willingness to change what is in the 'mind' or 'heart' that produces dis-ease to that which produces healing and health. One does not need to 'know' how to do this, or what specific changes need to be made, but only the willingness is needed.

So, what then is the role of the 'healer'?

The healer's role is to facilitate and reinforce the willingness, and to join with the person to be healed in requesting healing from Higher Power.

After that, the outcome is none of the 'healer's' concern.

HEALING IS ABOUT RE-ALIGNMENT.

It is about the willingness to re-direct the 'will' of the 'mind' or 'heart,' so it is in alignment, or more in alignment, with those Laws of the Universe and the Universal Mind governing health.

What about pills, surgery, laying-on-hands, massage, and other healing techniques?

Each of these things may be needed for 'setting the stage,' and to provide an atmosphere in which the individual seeking healing may be comfortable enough to allow the corrections to take place. These things are props and window dressing, though, and not the correction itself.

TWO WOLVES

An elder Cherokee Native American was teaching his grand-children about life. He said to them, "A fight is going on inside me ... it is a terrible fight and it is between two wolves.

"One wolf represents fear, anger, envy, sorrow, regret, greed, arrogance, self-pity, guilt, resentment, inferiority, lies, false pride, superiority, and ego.

"The other wolf stands for joy, peace, love, hope, sharing, serenity, humility, kindness, benevolence, friendship, empathy, generosity, truth, compassion, and faith.

"This same fight is going on inside you, and inside every other person, too."

The children thought about it for a minute and then one asked his Grandfather, "Which wolf will win?"

The old Cherokee simply replied, "The one you feed."

PEACE IS WITH YOU

We seem to have been searching for that Lasting Peace as though it were an item, a package, a commodity, a program, or a secret we could find somewhere 'out there,' then bring it home, so to speak, and put it inside ourselves.

Even when we experience Peace, we wonder where it came from, again looking outside, rather than within. We seek to recapture it, discover the formula, the origin, the trick, or the person who might have given it to us.

The Peace has always been there, within you. As have the Joy, Love, and Other Spiritual Attributes.

If you want to observe first-hand this is true, spend some time around an infant. They are at Peace most of the time. They lack a developed intellect, so they cannot tell us about it.

By the time they become adolescents, they have been taught and learned how to think thoughts that are not Peaceful, and which nearly 100% of the time block, cover up and obscure any awareness of Peace.

The road to re-discovery of the Peace lies in removing, replacing and changing those thoughts with which we prevent ourselves from experiencing 'Peace Is With Me.'

WISDOM

Wisdom. What is it? There perhaps have been many definitions of wisdom. It is something we think we recognize when we see it. Perhaps we recognize it in a grandfather who always seems to have the correct, on target, insightful comment at the right time. Perhaps it is a spiritual leader who inspires us.

It does not always come from those people who seem to have great intellects. In fact, often we see it in people who are otherwise quite ordinary.

Yet when asked to define what wisdom is, it seems very difficult to come up with an answer that really encompasses everything we internally identify as wisdom.

What is your definition of wisdom?

The best definition I have come across is, "Wisdom is intellect, lovingly applied, in search of more wisdom."

This phrase does not say 'great' intellect but just 'intellect.' Everybody has intellect of varying degrees. In fact, the phrase implies *any* intellect, 'lovingly applied, in search of more wisdom,' is wisdom.

The second part of the phrase - 'lovingly applied' - certainly hits home with me. I have seen, and I am sure you have, many people with above-average intellect who did not seem very wise and, in retrospect, perhaps that was because their intellect was not lovingly applied.

As to 'in search of more wisdom,' wisdom does not seem to stand still. There is a searching, a growing, an undercurrent of accumulation of more wisdom in those people who seem to be wise.

I am going to assume, correctly I am sure, you already have some intellect. I am also going to assume, because you are reading this, you are already searching.

The middle part of the definition of wisdom - the 'lovingly applied' part - refers to the style with which the intellect is imparted or given. Give it with 'win-win' in mind, or as though you are giving to self, to your own soul, with gentleness, yet with clarity and decisiveness.

Search often for opportunities to elevate your intellect to wisdom.

RECALL YOUR POWER

You are a philanthropist!

You have about 60,000 thoughts each day. You house them, feed them and protect them, no matter whether they are upsetting or not, in your best interest or not, old or new, or pertinent to today or not. And most importantly, you finance them daily with your energy. Feeling more tired lately?

Ever since you began accepting thoughts for storage into your mind, you had to create a little space for each, and supply it with a little daily allowance of your energy, for it to continue as part of your memory, whether conscious, subconscious, or unconscious.

Although some of these thoughts were your own creations, many were someone else's you accepted because it seemed the right thing to do at the time. Some even seemed homeless, for you didn't know where they came from. Still, you nurtured them all, at least for a time, and you rid yourself of few.

Now, with the application of the Thought Monitor, many more thoughts than usual are leaving and leaving rapidly, leaving empty spaces. Each space is also still supported by your energy. You gave your energy the assignment to support that space where the thought used to live but doesn't anymore. You may have even given your energy the assignment to build a supporting infrastructure, of links to other thoughts, attitudes and emotions, and to words, deeds and omissions. This framework now lies unused, at least temporarily, but a decision will soon be made, either intentionally or by default, to fill these spaces with other thoughts, or to dismantle the space and its infrastructure, and recall your energy. If the default mode is chosen, if you choose not to be active in deciding what happens to the now unused portion, then it is likely the banished thought, the old thought that recently left, will return and settle back into the familiar framework, only stronger than before.

It is your energy. It belongs to you. Your energy would be quite comfortable returning to you, to wait for a better assignment, if you are not ready to re-fill that space with a new thought.

You are in a process of un-doing right now. And right now, you cannot see far enough ahead to know what the extent of the un-doing will be, nor how much energy you will return to yourself. Likewise, you are uncertain just what the overall picture will look like when the majority of the un-doing is done, and uncertain of what rebuilding will be desired. Do not be in a rush to re-use this newfound energy; rather just enjoy it for now. To begin reconstruction now would surely interfere with the un-doing you are just beginning to learn about, and just beginning to make into a strong tool to carry with you through life.

When you monitor a thought, and you notice it disappears, gently but firmly call your energy back, affirm the assignment is finished and completed, invite the energy to return to your energy reservoir and rest a while.

Recall the energy from the space you created, and from the supporting structures, the communication lines, and the connections you made, and then the process will have been completed.

ABOUT THE AUTHOR

Dr. Fred Smith is the founder of Raise the Level of the Pond, a not-for-profit spiritual organization, author of *Conscious Concepts*. Raised in a small town in Montana, he received a typical Roman Catholic upbringing, attending a local Roman Catholic grade school, where his training for life was mostly religious and performance oriented, rather than spiritual and internal. He spent a lot of time daydreaming, both in school and out, nothing dramatic, just a lot of mindtime. His mother, who had pet descriptions for each of her children, called him "my little dreamer." His parents were supportive of his 'dreaming' but had few skills with which to deal with their son's 'inner space,' and his upbringing remained mostly task oriented.

In 1957, Fred enrolled in the local, all-boys, Catholic High School, where the teachers were members of the Jesuit Order. The curriculum contained demanding academics, and the behavioral expectations were high. In addition to religious training, spiritual concepts were emphasized, to which Fred had a natural attraction. Still testosterone levels were often high, and social skills sometimes low, so that he found himself in conflict with most schoolmates, teachers, authority figures, and some of his friends and neighbors with uncomfortable frequency. As with most teenagers, he regularly assumed that the blame for the conflicts lay with his adversaries.

In spite of these frequent conflicts, Fred still often found time for 'inner space' and reflection. One day in 1958, when he was 15 years old, during a quiet and reflective time, he suddenly realized that the common factor in these conflicts was *himself*. He was astonished. Thoughts came flooding in and, as he evaluated them, he came to several startling conclusions: (1) He had participated in the development of most of his conflicts with others; (2) The rest of the world was not always out of step; (3) That inner processes influence external behavior; (4) He had at least some control over his inner processes; (5) He noticed that this period of reflection and discovery was accompanied by a tremendous feeling of Freedom; (6) He realized that this feeling was the result of inner processes, not external behavior. At *that* moment, he decided to make 'inner exploration' a major part of his life, a part that remains major today. This discovery of the extent to which owning his inner processes could .influence his life was a delightful and pleasant experience, and continues as it expands.

Later he would begin to sort out which inner processes were mind, which were brain, and which were spirit. Since that time, he has constantly studied in the fields of religion, spirituality, psychology, metaphysics, and eventually, medicine. He became a Doctor of Medicine and, after receiving his M.D. degree, specialized in the field of Medical Neurology, which deals with the Brain and Nervous System, and worked in this field in private practice for twenty years. While practicing medicine, he expanded and refined his understanding of the brain, and how the mind and spirit operate through it, learning through his interaction with thousands of patients and their families.

Dr. Smith has developed personal Tools that have worked well for him, which he calls 'Conscious Concepts.' He has organized several of these Tools into a teaching curriculum presented in this book, arranged in the same sequence that he teaches his students, face-to-face. His students have found that understanding the interconnection of spirit/mind/ brain, and how they sometimes affect the body, to be very useful, and valuable daily. With the teaching Tools, he found that exploration of the inner self is: (1) Practical in daily life; (2) Easier than most people make it; (3) Simpler than most people make it; (4) Produces unexpected freedom; (5) Is easy to teach; and

(6) Is easy to learn.

Dr Smith has withdrawn from the formal practice of medicine in order to share his understanding, knowledge, and wisdom, on various topics, with individuals, groups, and over the Internet, with the intention of reaching a wider audience than would be otherwise possible. His journey has led him to be ordained as a minister, symbolic of the union of scientific and spiritual knowledge. He founded RAISE THE LEVEL OF THE POND, a not-for-profit spiritual learning center, dedicated to the promotion of "inner" growth, in as many individuals as are ready to receive it. It is a source of gratification to Dr. Smith that his students so often pass on that which they have found to be of benefit and value.

ABOUT
"RAISE THE LEVEL OF THE POND"

A SPIRITUAL CENTER. The *pond* is a metaphor for humanity. Each molecule of water represents a person or being. When a pebble, which represents an item of knowledge, wisdom or understanding is thrown into the pond, the whole pond is raised, every molecule, every being. The web site is dedicated to raising the level of the pond, 'one pebble at a time.'

This is an exploration of 'inner space,' regardless whatever 'outer space' you find yourself in. The topics chosen are practical and relevant to everyday life. The 'pebbles' offered may be used on a daily basis, or even minute to minute. The approaches at times may seem familiar, but more often will appear, in some respects, to be the opposite of what you have been taught, previously. Learning will range from simple and very easy, to simple yet requiring persistence and focus over a longer time. Still, they will be simple rather than complicated.

Since each pebble presented represents a culmination of growth at the point it was written or given, it may appear to represent a *synthesis* of more than one system of thought, which it is. Understanding is drawn from the scientific world, from everyday life, and from spiritual teachings in order to bring greater consistency and integration to the processes of mind, and to promote a state in which 'outer' behaviors more closely reflect 'inner' processes.

In terms of *mission,* RAISE THE LEVEL OF THE POND is a spiritual organization that recognizes mind/body/spirit inter-connectedness, and that an individual may make improvements in mind, or body, or spirit, and that such improvements in one category may cause improvements in the other two. Our focus is on spiritual improvements (and often this requires adjusting a person's mind-set in order to remove barriers to spiritual growth). When spiritual growth occurs, sometimes a person will experience greater well-being in the areas of the physical and the emotional, and these are welcome side-effects of the spiritual learning and growth. Our focus is on the practical aspects of spirituality, those that can be used and applied routinely, without imposing any need to change external appearances, beyond what comes as a natural consequence to internal changes.

www.ingramcontent.com/pod-product-compliance
Lightning Source LLC
Chambersburg PA
CBHW061708120626
46550CB00003B/1147